THE ALCÁZAR
OF SEGOVIA

EDICIONES
Aldeasa

MAP OF THE ALCAZAR

Entrance

THE ALCAZAR
OF SEGOVIA

Aldeasa

THE KINGS OF THE ALCÁZAR

Alfonso VIII *He of Las Navas* (1158-1214) - Eleonore of England

Alfonso IX of León (1171-1230) - **Berenguela of Castile**

Ferdinand III *the Saint* (1217-1252) - Beatrice of Swabia

Alfonso X *the Wise* (1252-1284) - Violante of Aragon

Sancho IV *the Brave* (1284-1295) - María de Molina

Ferdinand IV *the Summoned* (1295-1312) - Constance of Portugal

Mary of Portugal - **Alfonso XI** *the Just* (1312-1350) - mistress Leonor de Guzmán

Peter I *the Cruel* (1350-1369)   Juana Manuel - **Henry II** (1369-1379)

John I (1379-1390) - Eleonore of Aragon

Catherine of Lancaster - **Henry III** *the Sufferer* (1390-1406)

Mary of Aragon   -   **John II** (1406-1454)   -   Isabella of Portugal

Henry IV *the Impotent* (1454-1474)   **Isabella** *the Catholic* (1474-1504) - Ferdinand of Aragon

Joan I *the Mad* (1504-1517) - Philip *the Handsome* of Austria

Charles V (1517-1556)- Isabella of Portugal

Philip II (1556-1598) - Anna of Austria

Philip III (1598-1621) - Margaret of Inner Austria

Philip IV (1637-1665) - Maria Anna of Austria

Charles II (1665-1700)

Bourbon Dynasty (1700-)

María Luisa of Savoy - **Philip V** (1700-1746)   -   Isabella of Parma

Louis I (1724)   **Ferdinand VI** (1746-1758)

Charles III (1759-1788) - Maria Amalia of Saxony

Charles IV (1788-1808) - Maria Luisa of Parma

Ferdinand VII (1814-1833) - Maria Cristina of the Two Sicilies

Isabella II (1833-1868) - Francisco de Asis

Alfonso XII (1875-1885) - Maria Cristina of Austria

Alfonso XIII (1902-1931) - Victoria Eugenia of Battenberg

(Opposite) View of the Alcázar from the banks of the Eresma.

THE PALACE OF THE KINGS OF CASTILE

The Alcázar of Segovia is not only one of most popular attractions in Spain but, due to its shape – that of a ship – also one of the most unique. Before entering its gate, it is well worthwhile to recall its fascinating history and the various functions which, over the centuries and according to the dictates of each age, it has performed. Originally a fortress, it has served as a royal palace, a state prison, a Royal Artillery College and, more recently, a military academy.

The upper part of the city has been of major strategic importance since Roman times, proof of this being that the system of water distribution from the Aqueduct extends as far as the Alcázar's moat. Although Segovia was repopulated in the reign of Alfonso VI *the Brave* (1072-1109) in the late 11th century, the first record of the building is an early 12th-century document referring to a fortress on the River Eresma. By the Middle Ages this fortress had become known as the "Alcázar" – an Arabic word used to describe all royal residences. Due to the beauty of its setting, its impregnability, and its proximity to the famous Guadarrama forest hunting preserves, the Alcázar became one of the favourite residences of the kings of Castile.

The oldest existing part of the palace-fortress dates from the time of the transition from Romanesque to Gothic. If, as is thought, the two floors built on the rock close to the Eresma date from the reign of Alfonso VIII *"He of Las Navas"* (1158-1214), then the two large towers raised to defend the palace to the east and west also date from that period.

The palace was extended on a large scale by the monarchs of the Trastámara dynasty, some of whom were fascinated by Eastern art. This is clearly evident in the Alcázar's lofty coffered ceilings with their multicoloured ornamental bows, and the dados and friezes in which late-Gothic charm blends with the geometry of Arabic decoration.

The Alcázar's time of greatest splendour came in the reign of **John II** (1405-1454), when a number of new projects were implemented, including the addition of the small towers and the enlargement of the so-called **East Tower** and the **moat**. When still a prince, John's son ordered the friezes and ceiling of the **Pine-cone Room** built, and subsequently, as king Henry IV *the Impotent* (1454-1474), commissioned the friezes and dome for the **Throne Room**. Henry is also attributed with the completion of the frieze in the **Hall of the Kings** and the decoration of the **Cord Room**. Through the Accord of Toros de Guisando Henry acknowledged his sister Isabella the Catholic (1474-1504) as his heiress and on his death she was proclaimed queen. However, after Isabella and Ferdinand of Aragon were secretly married in 1469, he revoked the treaty and acknowledged the legitimacy of his daughter Joan, called *La Beltraneja* as she was rumoured to be the illegitimate daughter of the Queen's favourite, Beltrán de la Cueva.

The Alcázar played a crucial role in Isabella's proclamation as queen: when

(Opposite) The Proclamation of Isabella the Catholic as Queen of Castile and León *(detail)* by *Muñoz de Pablos. Galley Room.*

news reached Segovia on 12th December 1474 that the king had died the previous day in Madrid, *Doña* Isabella hurried to take refuge within the walls of this, the greatest fortress in Castile, where she received the support of the governor, Andrés Cabrera, and the consensus of the Segovia council. The next day – the feast of St Lucy and that of her coronation as Queen of Castile and León – two of the councillors led the horse she rode while others held a brocade canopy over her. The cortege then proceeded to the Plaza de San Miguel, where Isabella was crowned and, on the new queen's return, Cabrera delivered the Alcázar into her possession, thus consolidating her sovereignty of all Castile and León.

Under Philip II (1558-1598) major alterations were made to the Alcázar's interior and the layout of the rooms was rearranged; the king's first concern, however, was to remedy the ruinous state into which the palace had fallen. It was also during Philip's reign that the slate-covered roofs and the spires of the towers that are so characteristic of the fortress (and are unique in Spain) were added. The king's marriage to his fourth wife, Anna of Austria, in 1570 was the last great historic event to which the Alcázar served as a setting.

Rule of Spain by the Bourbon dynasty began under Philip V (1700-1746), who was named heir by his childless uncle, Charles II. The Bourbons preferred the forests of the Guadarrama mountains to the Segovia countryside, although Charles III (1759-1788) was responsible for a radical change which affected the destiny of the old palace, for he judged it the perfect place in which to found a military college for young cadets in the Royal Artillery Corps. The College was solemnly inaugurated on 16th May 1764, the Alcázar serving as its headquarters for almost a century – until on 6th March 1862 a fierce blaze destroyed almost all of the ceilings. Since then the College – known as the Royal Artillery College and regarded not only as Spain's foremost military academy but one of the best in Europe – has been based in the old Monastery of San Francisco.

The fire of 1862 may have been started by sparks of soot from a stove in the first master's office, now the **Queen's Boudoir**. A strong wind may then have fanned the flames, causing them to spread quickly so that in the space of a few hours all the ceilings were destroyed. Part of the **Tower of John II** was also damaged and the only spire to remain intact was that on the left turret.

Restoration of the Alcázar began under **Alfonso XII** (1875-1886). The work was completed in 1896 during the regency of Queen Maria Cristina and on 22nd January of that year, the Alcázar and its grounds, outbuildings and annexes was ceded by royal order to the Royal Artillery. Subsequently, by a royal decree of 18th January 1951, a Board of Trustees was set up to ensure that the restoration and adaptation of the interior was continued.

The Gardens and the Projecting Façade

The Alcázar entrance is a gate built in 1817 during the reign of Ferdinand VII

(Opposite) The Heroes of 2nd May memorial.

(1814-1833). The esplanade beyond (where a *Romanesque Cathedral*, demolished after the War of the Communities, stood until the 16th century) is known as the Plaza de la Reina Victoria Eugenia in commemoration of a visit by Alfonso XIII and his wife Queen Victoria Eugenia in 1908 to celebrate the first centenary of the 2nd May uprising. The area was converted into gardens on the occasion of Philip II's marriage to Anna of Austria, his fourth wife. At the centre stands a **memorial** to Daoíz and Velarde, former pupils of the Royal Artillery College and **heroes of the May 2nd uprising.**

Known as the **"Chemistry House"**, the Neo-Classical building to the left of the Alcázar was inaugurated in 1792 as the Artillery College laboratory. Since 1898 it has housed the General Military Archive.

The great height of the Tower of John II is accentuated by the **moat**, which was dug over various periods during the Middle Ages. The moat is spanned by an arcade dating from the 16th century and crossed by means of a drawbridge whose raising mechanism can still be seen. The lintel above the granite main entrance displays a large coat of arms bearing the emblems of all the states which formed Philip II's realm surrounded by the collar and insignia of the Order of the Golden Fleece. Both the tower and the rest of the building are adorned with *sgraffito*, a decorative technique of geometric designs in two layers.

The Tower of John II

Before entering the building, it is a good idea to halt before the imposing Tower of John II. About halfway up the wall, a line of balls marks the tower's original height when it was the *East Tower*. The barred windows recall the tower's long period as a prison. On the lower level, the beautiful double horseshoe-arch window with a brick moulding rising from a stone base is Almohad and dates from the 13th century.

Reached from the castle entrance, the tower rises in four levels and has 156 steps, the final section leading to a large terrace with a splendid view of the surrounding area: in the foreground the city's Canonjías district; to the right and next to the Cathedral, the old Jewish Quarter with the Jewish cemetery on the banks of the River Clamores opposite it; to the left the Eresma Valley and the Church of La Veracruz; and in the distance the *Sierra de Guadarrama* (with Peñalara the highest peak) and the mountain known as "La Mujer Muerta", famous for its shape of a recumbent woman.

The Tower of John II is the result of the extension of the East Tower, a project begun during John's reign in the 15th century and completed by the architect Juan Guas in the reign of the Catholic Monarchs (whose ciphers are displayed on one of the merlons).

The tower was once a prison from which there was virtually no means of escape as only a narrow passageway known as **"Executioner's Alley"** crosses this turreted mass of stone with its incredibly thick walls. There is no record of any execution at the Alcázar, however. The tower's illustrious prisoners

(Pages 10 and 11) View of the Alcázar.
(Opposite) The Plaza de la Reina Victoria Eugenia and the façade of the Tower of John II.

enjoyed certain comforts in their cells – tapestries, carpets, furniture, etc. – in accordance with their rank. The last "state prisoner" was Alfonso XIII's prime minister, General Berenguer, who was incarcerated by the government of the Second Republic.

The Cellars

A corridor to the right of the entrance to the first courtyard leads to the cellar stairs. In the cellars themselves, the Roman remains which form part of the Alcázar's foundations are clearly visible, as is the rock itself, which is honeycombed with caves and tunnels (used in time of war as secret passages).

The *Patio de Armas*

The *Patio de Armas* or "parade ground courtyard" is the centre of distribution to the fortress and owes its present form to alterations made in the reign of Philip II (1556-1598). Designed by Francisco de Mora in the El Escorial architectural style of which Philip was so fond, it was built in 1593. The two-storey building around the courtyard is of granite, its lower gallery formed by semi-circular arches on slender pillars and the upper surmounted with lintels. Recent restoration work has revealed remains of geminated windows of the same type as the early 13th-century ones on the north side of the palace. Remains of semi-circular arches (some slightly pointed) in the Romanesque-Gothic transitional style have also been discovered.

The large stone coat of arms at the centre of the south wall was originally positioned over the main entrance. The heraldic devices – the fleece and Portuguese shields – are those of Philip II as King of Portugal. Two basins which blend in harmoniously with their architectural surroundings and a fountain at the centre complete the ornamentation of the courtyard. Busts of Charles I and Philip II (copies of originals by Pompeo Leoni) and of Philip III and Charles III have recently been added at the back to the courtyard.

In the west corner, a flight of Herreran-style stairs leads to the upper floor and the main rooms of the General Military Archive. In the same corner and by the door to the **Royal Artillery College Museum** are a mortar dating from 1487 and another cannon cast in 1797.

The Royal Artillery College Museum

The museum entrance is situated in the right-hand corner of the parade ground. The coat of arms of the Royal Artillery College was placed above the doorway in 1764.

After Philip II's new layout, none of the rooms in this area retained their original appearance except those on the north wing. Recent restoration work has revealed a geminated window similar to those in the Old Palace Hall which now offers a fine view of the beautiful Clamores Valley. In compliance with a decree issued by the Alcázar's Board of Trustees, these three rooms (open to the public) now belong to the Royal Artillery College.

(Opposite) The Patio de Armas *with the Tower of John II at the back.*

Heading the portraits of "illustrious sons" of the Royal College are those of its founder *Charles III* (a copy of an original by Mengs) and the first director *Count Felix Gazzola de Cereto* (a copy of an original by Molinareto from the Gazzola de Piacenza Foundation). The College's most famous old boys are Captains Luis Daoíz and Pedro Velarde, heroes of the uprising of 2nd May 1808. A chart at the entrance illustrates the various periods in the College's history.

Also exhibited are items dating from the Peninsular War and the Napoleonic invasion. Of special interest in the display cabinets are a number of weapons, text books, documents, autograph albums and tableware from the Seville Charterhouse.

The museum also commemorates the College's history over the almost one hundred years when the Alcázar served as its headquarters. Each space is divided up in the following way: display cabinets at the centre of the room, examples of artillery techniques along the right wall and of tactics along the left. Information is displayed on the exhibits in each section.

The Old Palace Hall

Dating from the time of the original Alcázar of Alfonso VIII (1158-1214, known as "He of Las Navas" after his victory over the Almohads at the Battle of Navas de Tolosa in 1212), this room is now known as the **Geminated Window Room** due to the four *miradors* in its north wall. For centuries these large

balconies which once faced the exterior were hidden from view, having been walled up to form a partition between the room and a new extension. They display features typical of the Cistercian style of the early 13th century, while the walls at the sides of the geminated windows were decorated in the 12th century with red on white stucco.

In the original fortress, this room was known as the "Palacio Maior" and was an audience room. In the Middle Ages, this and the two smaller rooms flanking it formed the palace area. The room to the left was the **Royal Chamber** or monarchs' bedroom, while that to the right served as an antechamber to the throne room and was known as the **Fireplace Room.** A small stairway next to the door of the Royal Chamber and leading down to the cellars was used by the guards at the changing of the night watch inside the palace.

The bards and suits of armour were made in the German style of the 15th and 16th centuries, while the halberds date from the reign of Ferdinand VII.

The Fireplace Room

This room takes its name from the fireplace (dating from the reign of Philip II) in the south wall. Its general appearance is reminiscent of the king's rooms at the Monastery of El Escorial. The granite fireplace is said to contain ashlars taken from the aqueduct during alterations.

Great care has also been taken to reproduce the kind of furniture typical of

(Opposite) Horse armour. Old Palace Hall.

Philip II's residences. The items include: monk's chairs, a bench with scenes of the martyrdom of St Lawrence carved on the back, a secretaire with small painted gilt columns, and a number of mirrors similar to those in Velázquez's painting *Las Meninas*.

The walls are graced with 17th-century landscape paintings of imaginary palaces and gardens, although one depicts the original Alcázar next to the old cathedral (destroyed during the War of the Communities). Also displayed are a Flemish tapestry of *The Marriage of Mary and Joseph* and copies of portraits of *Philip II* (from an original by Pantoja de la Cruz) and *Philip III* (from an original by Titian). The hearth displays an iron plaque with the coat of arms of the first Bourbons. The doors are flanked by halberds. As in all the rooms in the area that are open to the public, the dado tiling is 19th-century and in the Talavera style.

The Throne Room

This room formed part of the extension built by the Trastámara kings. According to an inscription commemorating *The Battle of Jimena* below the frieze, the decoration dates from the reign of Henry IV (15th century).

The adornment of the door leading to the Fireplace Room is completely intact. The original stucco frieze is of interlacing circles – a common Segovian Mudéjar motif. The painted wooden dome bears scenes of chivalry and wild animals, motifs very popular at the time of its construction. This dome replaced the original one, which

was completely destroyed in the fire of 1862. From a church in Urones de Castroponce in Tierra de Campos, it dates from the same period and was made by the same craftsman – the Mudéjar master Xadel Mayor.

The thrones and velvet canopy were made especially for the visit to the Alcázar by Alfonso XIII (1902-1931) and Queen Victoria Eugenia on the occasion of the centenary of the May 2nd uprising. They are the only monarchs to have used the thrones. As this area commemorates the Catholic Monarchs, the canopy trimming bears Isabella and Ferdinand's coat of arms with the motto "Tanto Monta". The royal arms behind the thrones rest on the eagle of St John.

The portraits of the Catholic Monarchs – Queen *Isabella* by Madrazo and King *Ferdinand* by Montañer – date from the 19th century. In the large stained-glass window, Henry IV, on horseback, is likened to St James "the Moorslayer". All the windows were made by the Segovian artist Muñoz de Pablos, who took his inspiration for the figures from the *Kings of Castile Codex* compiled by Hernando de Avila, court painter to Philip II.

The Galley Room

When the Old Palace was extended, the Galley Room became the principal room in the Alcázar. Its name comes from its huge ceiling in the form of an inverted ship's hull. The original ceiling was built by order of Queen Catherine of Lancaster, widow of Henry *the Sufferer*, when regent during the minority of her

(Opposite) The Throne Room.

son, John II, but it was destroyed in the fire of 1862. Its reconstruction was possible thanks to drawings made by Avrial before the fire in 1847. The wall between the Galley Room and the Throne Room was also destroyed in the fire and was subsequently rebuilt.

In the Mudéjar frieze, the arms of Castile and León alternate with ornamental bows running between two inscriptions, the upper with the date (1412) when the frieze was installed and the lower with the prayer *Anima Christi*, then popular at the Court of Castile.

Before the construction of the new rooms, the front facing wall of the old palace hall was exterior, which explains its four geminated windows. The masonry still displays the adornment (with small pieces of mineral scoria at the intersections) which gave rise to the later *sgraffito* work.

At the end of the room is a large painting of *The Proclamation of Isabella the Catholic as Queen of Castile and León* in reference to an event which took place in the atrium of the Church of San Miguel in Segovia on 13th December 1474. As models for the figures in the scene, Muñoz de Pablos recruited contemporaries who frequented the Alcázar, some being descendants of those who had actually been present at the coronation.

Two embroidered tapestries on crimson velvet (a reproduction of a series of Roman emperors from the Monastery of Las Huelgas) flank the door leading to the Throne Room. The room also contains various suits of armour.

The figures depicted in the stained-glass windows are kings of Castile. At the centre of one is the founder of the Trastámara dynasty, Henry II (1369-1379, called *"He of the Largesse"* due to the generosity he was forced to show towards the nobles in order to retain the throne), while the section to the left depicts the death of Peter I *the Cruel* (1350-1369) at the hands of his stepbrother, Henry Trastámara, and that to the right the death of Henry's son, John I, as the result of a fall from a horse. The coats of arms are those of Castile and León (beneath Henry II), and of Aragon (beneath John I) while those with dragon's heads (beneath Peter I) are a Trastámara emblem. In the other window, Henry III (1390-1406, known as *the Sufferer* due to his constant ill-health) appears on the throne of Aragon accompanied by his wife and children, the infantes.

From this room a balcony with a large ogive overlooking the Eresma Valley offers one of the most beautiful views of Segovia with, from left to right: the shrine of Our Lady of La Fuencisla (patron saint of the city and province of Segovia); the Monastery of Discalced Carmelites (the site of St John's tomb); at the highest point, the village of Zamarramala (famous for the feast of St Agatha, when for one day each year the women take control of the municipality); the Church of La Vera Cruz; and the Monastery of El Parral y La Ceca.

The Pine-cone Room

This room takes its name from the decorative motif on the ceiling, where 392 pine-cones – all different – are displayed. As in the Throne Room, the

(Opposite) The coffered ceiling in the Pine-cone Room.

frieze is Gothic with features of Mudéjar design in the composition. The four angels bear shields with the arms of Castile and León. The inscription on the frieze relates that the room was adorned in 1452 by order of Henry IV when he was heir to the throne.

Inspired like all the others in the building by the codex mentioned above, the stained-glass window in this room depicts the Alcázar's founder, Alfonso VIII, with his daughter Lady Berenguela. The heraldry refers to the kingdom of Castile only, this being Alfonso's exclusive possession. The crimson damask-covered walls are graced with Flemish tapestries dating from the 15th and 16th centuries. Of great interest among the items of furniture is a gilded and painted 17th-century vargueno cabinet. The small windows in this room still display the ravages of the fire of 1862.

The Royal Chamber

This chamber, which was the king's bedroom, accommodated Ferdinand VII (1814-1833) during his visit to the artillery college in 1817. The mouldings adorning the Mudéjar Gothic doors are copies in Novelda stone of stuccos from the Palace of Henry IV in Segovia's San Martín district. The walls are hung with tapestries depicting court and tourney scenes during the reign of the Catholic Monarchs. The ceiling displays the shields and arms of the kings of Castile and León. Divided by the arms of Castile and León, the arms of Joan of Portugal are displayed on the screens.

Above the door to the old palace is an effigy of St Anthony.

The walnut bed is Gothic and dates from the 16th century. It has a crimson brocade canopy woven in gold and the quilt, which is also of brocade, displays the arms of Castile and León as they were in the reign of Henry IV.

The Hall of the Kings

The principal room in the castle, the Hall of the Kings served as a venue for the most important court ceremonies. Although its construction is attributed to Alfonso X *the Wise* (1252-1284) there is no documentary evidence to actually support such a claim. The drawings and paintings display all the features typical of the late-Gothic period and of Philip II's restoration. As the original room was completely destroyed in the fire of 1862, it was necessary to refer to the *Kings of Castile Codex* and to Avrial's drawings when it was reconstructed.

The ceiling is formed by Renaissance-influenced hexagonal coffers. Reminiscent of choir stalls, the frieze contains fifty-two effigies of all the kings and queens of Asturias, León and Castile from Pelayo (720-737) to Joan *the Mad* (1504-1517). The cartouches were composed by Esteban Garibay and refer to the most important events in each monarch's reign.

Extremely curious is the numbering of the kings with the name Alfonso, for it differs from that used in the history books. The first change comes with Alfonso I of Aragon, who is listed as Alfonso VII, husband of Doña Urraca, daughter of

(Pages 22 and 23) The Royal Chamber. (Opposite) View of the Hall of the Kings with The Conquest of Cadiz by Alfonso the Wise by Bejarano (top), and a view of the Hall of the Kings (bottom).

Alfonso VI of Castile and León. Consequently Alfonso X *the Wise* appears as Alfonso XI. Likewise the names of the queens are numbered in chronological order, so that Isabella *the Catholic* becomes Isabella VI and her daughter, Joan I *the Mad*, Joan VII.

On a lower level, four niches above the side doors contain the images of Fernán González (first Count of Castile), El Cid Campeador and Counts Raymond of Burgundy and Henry of Lorraine, sons-in-law of Alfonso VI (1072-1109), the first king to repopulate the city.

The decoration is completed with Bejarano's painting *The Conquest of Cadiz by Alfonso the Wise* and copies of portraits of *Philip II*, his fourth wife *Anna of Austria*, and Queen *Elizabeth of France*, Philip IV's (1621-1665) first wife. The wooden seats were made especially for Alfonso XIII's visit to the Alcázar.

A cross set in the floor of this room's large balcony commemorates Henry II's son, Pedro, who on that spot fell to his death from his governess's arms. Terrified by what had happened, the governess threw herself after him. The infant was buried in the old cathedral, but his tomb was later transferred to the new cathedral, for whose custody the king granted the chapter the "privilege of the two mace-bearers".

The Cord Room

This room was restored in the early 20th century in the Henry IV style according to Avrial's drawings. Interesting is the unusual coffered ceiling of pavilions painted with a starry-sky motif. The frieze, which was originally in relief, has been painted to reproduce scenes of chivalry. The north wall consists of a gallery of basket-handle arches with a worked slate safety parapet. The south wall is graced with a tapestry with details of the *Capture of Arcila* series (the original being in the Collegiate Church of Pastrana in Guadalajara). The decoration of this small room is completed with a predella of saints and martyrs from a Gothic altar and various early 16th-century panels of religious themes, including *The Annunciation*, *St Barbara* and *St Lucy*.

The room's most interesting feature, however, is the frieze decoration, which represents the *cord of St Francis*. According to legend, Alfonso X the Wise ordered it placed around the room in atonement for blasphemously boasting that the universe would be far better if God had conferred with him before creating it. According to a chronicler of the times, God punished Alfonso for his audacity by sending a bolt of lightning which rocked the strong building, humbling the king and spurring him to atonement. However, the decorative motif is more probably due to Henry IV, who also ceded a country estate near the city to the Franciscans. Known as San Antonio el Real, the estate now houses a community of Poor Clares.

A wooden latticed screen dividing a small adjacent room from the Chapel allowed the monarchs to hear mass separately from the court.

(Opposite) View of the Chapel and its 16th-century altarpiece.

The Queen's Boudoir

Once known as the "King's water closet", this small chamber stands adjacent to the Cord Room. It was almost certainly here where the fire broke out. The ceiling, which, according to the old descriptions, originally consisted of four coffers adorned with blue and gold, was also completely destroyed by the flames and was replaced by a flat one with vegetal motifs. The dado is of 16th-century Toledo tilework.

The Chapel

In was in this chapel where the ceremony of the veil was performed after Philip II's marriage to Anna of Austria. Although decorated in the Renaissance style before the fire, it now displays a Mudéjar coffered ceiling from a Church in Cedillo de la Torre in the province of Segovia. The walls are covered with damask bearing a pattern of shells and the cross of St James – both emblems of the saint. The dado is of ancient Talavera tilework. The backs of two Renaissance stalls in the choir are carved with heads of the Catholic Monarchs. The stained-glass windows display figures of saints traditionally associated with the royal family of Castile.

The high altarpiece, which dates from the first quarter of the 16th century, is from the school of Valladolid and consists of seventeen panels with scenes from the New Testament. The entablature, which was acquired by the Board of Trustees in 1962, is Gothic Plateresque and came from the parish church of Viana de Cega. At the centre stands a Gothic wood-carving of *St Barbara* (patron saint of artillerymen), and in a niche to the left is another – Romanesque – figure of the saint recently discovered during restoration work. In front of the altarpiece is a silver processional cross and on the floor, in the centre of the room, the tombs of two former Alcázar treasurers.

The altarpiece in the north wall dates from the 15th century and was made by the school of Castile. The central panel depicts *St James the Moorslayer with a Pilgrim's Hat*, while to the sides are saints *Sebastian, Agatha, Vincent and Bridget*. Opposite the altarpiece is one of the few works of art saved from the flames, an *Adoration of the Magi* signed by Bartolommeo Carducci in 1600. Another magnificent work in the chapel is a *Descent from the Cross* by Seghers.

The Ante-chapel

A 16th-century wrought-iron screen from the workshop of Cristóbal de Andino separates the chapel and ante-chapel. This room, whose dado is adorned with Talavera tilework, leads to the Clock Courtyard and, via the door on the right, to the **Well Terrace.**

The Clock Courtyard

The decoration and architecture in this area is simpler than in the parade ground (reached from this point via a vaulted

(Opposite) The Clock Courtyard (top), and the Weapons Room (bottom).

passageway at the far end). This courtyard takes its name from the sun dial on the tower wall, which leads to the **Keep** stairs. The imperial coat of arms of Charles I above the door was removed from San Martín's gate when it was demolished at the end of the 19th century. Below the Keep is the Armoury.

The Weapons Room or Armoury

Despite the famous fire of 1862, the structure of this room (whose barrel vault displays all the features typical of the 13th-century Cistercian style of architecture) remained intact. As the castle ends in the shape of a ship's prow, this last room is wedge-shaped. In the walls to either side are large geminated windows, one overlooking the Clamores Valley and the small hill where the mediaeval Jewish cemetery is situated, while the other overlooks the passageway to the King's Terrace.

This room formerly contained the most important items from the royal armoury and the king's treasury. Today it houses a noteworthy collection of weapons, mortars, pikes, halberds, bombards, culverins, lances and, most importantly, rapiers dating from the 15th to the 17th century. A number of the coats of armour are beautifully damascened, but perhaps the most interesting exhibit of all is the *hunting cross-bow adorned with the imperial eagle* in the display cabinet. It is similar to that depicted in Lucas Cranach's portrait of the Emperor Charles V (now in the Museo del Prado).

The Treasury

This small semi-circular chamber at the base of the Keep was the storehouse for the most valuable items in the king's treasury. The grating at the entrance is Romanesque. The *press* at the centre of the room is made of bronze and weighs 4,292 pounds. It was used for minting coins in the reign of the first Bourbon king, Philip V. To the side, three strongboxes with complicated mechanisms – one with fourteen springs – are fine examples of the magnificent work of the craftsmen of the Segovia Mint, founded by Philip II in the 16th century.

The Well Terrace, Almohad Garden and Flanking Tower

This terrace takes its name from a well at the centre dating from the reign of Philip II. It also offers a view of the Keep (the Alcázar's most famous tower) in all its splendour. To the left and below is the **Almohad Garden**, also known as the Patio de la Fruta ("Courtyard of the Fruit"), whose layout is reproduced on the coffered ceiling in the Galley Room. The garden can be seen only from this point. A stairway from the terrace leads down to the **Flanking Tower,** originally a watchtower over the Clamores Valley.

(Opposite) The Well Terrace.

© ALDEASA, 2004

I.S.B.N.: 84-8003-223-5

Legal deposit: M-22185-2004

Photographs: © Archivo Aldeasa
              José Barea

Published and produced by: ALDEASA

Written by: Natalia San Martín González

Translation: Nigel Williams

Collection design: A. Ochoa de Zabalegui

Layout: Myriam López Consalvi

Photomechanical production: Lucam

Printed by: Jomagar

Cover: View of the Alcázar.

Back cover: The Henry II window. Galley Room